EASY HOME IMPROVEMENTS

your child's bedroom

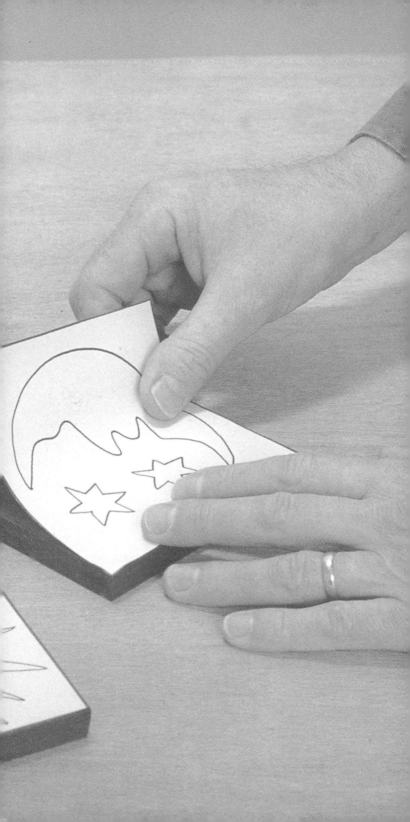

EASY HOME
IMPROVEMENTS

your child's bedroom

STEWART WALTON

LEBHAR-FRIEDMAN BOOKS

New York • Chicago • Los Angeles • London • Paris • Tokyo

Lebhar-Friedman Books
425 Park Avenue
New York, NY 10022

First U.S. edition published 2001 by Lebhar-Friedman Books
Copyright © 2000 Marshall Editions Ltd, London, U.K.

Published by Lebhar-Friedman Books
Lebhar-Friedman Books is a company of Lebhar-Friedman, Inc.

Printed and bound in China by Excel Printing.
Originated in Singapore by Pica.

Library of Congress Cataloging-in-Publication Data
on file at the Library of Congress.
ISBN: 0-86730-835-4

Project Editor Guy Croton
Designer Glen Wilkins
Editorial Coordinator Caroline Watson
Photographer Alistair Hughes
Managing Editor Antonia Cunningham
Managing Art Editor Phil Gilderdale
Editorial Director Ellen Dupont
Editorial Coordinator Ros Highstead
Art Director Dave Goodman
Production Amanda Mackie
Indexer Adam Richard

Front cover photography: **Stewart Grant/Robert
Harding Picture Library**
Back cover photography: **Alistair Hughes**

Visit our Web site at lfbooks.com

Volume Discounts
This book makes a great gift and incentive. Call (212) 756-5240
for information on volume discounts.6

Note

Every effort has been taken to ensure that all information in this book
is correct and compatible with national standards generally accepted at
the time of publication. For the photographs in this book, both power
and hand tools have been positioned as a guide only. Always follow the
manufacturer's instructions for any tools, and wear protective clothing
and apparatus where recommended. The author and publisher disclaim
any liability, loss, injury or damage incurred as a consequence, directly
or indirectly, of the use and application of the contents of this book.
None of the material in this book may be reproduced without the
permission of Marshall Developments Ltd.

contents

introduction

Your child's bedroom is a very important place. It is the first room they will ever spend much time in, and the space in which they will begin to assert their individual personality most strongly. It needs to offer a warm and comforting yet stimulating and interesting ambience all at the same time. It must be a room in which the child can sleep in comfort and security, play with cheerful abandon and study or create in a conducive environment.

Perhaps the easiest way to ensure that your child will be happy in their personal space is to decorate it in an appealing, fun manner. Children like bright colors and strong patterns, so you could try the multicolored daisy stencils on pages 10–15 or the sun and moon-stamped roller blind that follows later in Chapter 1. Alternatively, there is a rather special set of wooden picket window shutters on pages 24–31 that would bring an individual touch to any room.

All children have toys—very often, *lots* of toys—and these require plenty of storage space. Many of the projects in this book have been included with this universal truth in mind. The underbed storage drawer on pages 42–49 offers an attractive and imaginative solution to a shortage of space and is not difficult to construct. Similarly, the decorated wooden toybox on pages 58–67 will serve as a good catch-all for small toys and will also look good in any child's bedroom. Its lid can be personalized with the name or initials of your child to enhance the sense of personal territory and belonging that every children's room should offer.

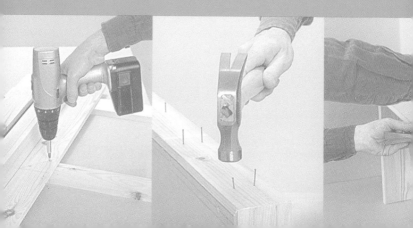

If the practical consideration of storage space is important to you, then what it contains—the toys themselves —is even more important to your child. At the heart of this book are ideas for several traditional wooden toys that will delight your son or daughter, from the oven play-cupboard on pages 68–77 to the doll's house on pages 94–101. These projects require fairly good woodworking skills to construct, but they are well worth the effort involved. Finally, the book is rounded-off with several projects that double as both toys and practical items at the same time. The television-screen fun mirror on pages 102–7 is a good example of this versatility, as is the delightful appliqué-cat bed quilt also found in chapter 3.

The projects in this book were designed to be accessible to as wide a range of people as possible, so none of them are especially difficult to make. Each project is graded with a skill rating of "Beginner," "Intermediate," or "Advanced," to help you select the items most suited to your own abilities. They are also backed-up with a rough indication of how long the project should take to make and full details of all the materials and tools required. With careful attention to any manufacturer's instructions and standard safety precautions, and the use of good quality tools and protective clothing, you should not encounter any real difficulties in constructing something special and a little different for your child's bedroom. Who knows, maybe one day your child will proudly pass on your handywork to their own children. Enjoy these projects.

Stewart Walton

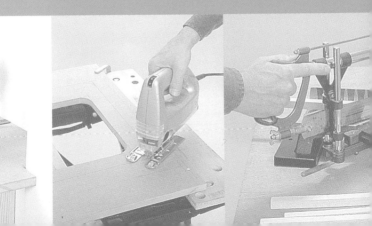

Walls & windows

making
daisy stencils

Stencilling is an ancient art that offers limitless possibilities for decorating walls. It is so easy to vary the colors and sizes of stencils to create a wealth of different decorative effects. These daisy stencils are simple to make and relatively straightforward to plan out in a pattern on the wall. Experiment with their scale to suit the size of your child's bedroom, and consider using them to brighten any room that has poor lighting or a reduced aspect. This is one project that you could let your child share in with you, with a little careful supervision!

Materials
2 pieces of stencil card or mylar • Low-tack spray adhesive • Selection of acrylic or water-based paint colors

Tools
Scalpel/craft knife • Plumb line—string, bluetack and a key for the weight • Cutting mat • Rule with integral spirit level • 2 medium-sized white plates • Pencil • 2 stencil brushes

Skill level
Beginner

Time
4 hours

1 Copy the stencil template on page 108 of this book, enlarging it on a photocopier. Copy or draw your stencil pattern to the size that you want, making two separate drawings, one of the center circle and one of the petals. Cut a square around the drawings so that they are 2 in. shorter on each side than the two pieces of stencil card.

2 Apply low-tack spray adhesive to one or both surfaces (according to the manufacturer's instructions), and press the pattern onto the card, smoothing from the center outward. Make sure there are no air bubbles trapped between the pattern and the card. You can stick the patterns either to the sheets of stencil card or, alternatively, to clear plastic (mylar). Leave a margin of at least 2 in. of card or mylar around the outside of the designs.

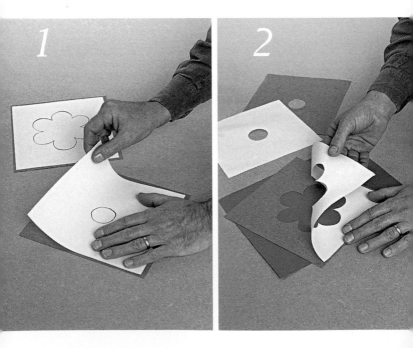

3 Allow the adhesive to dry, then place the stencil cards on a piece of scrap plywood or a cutting mat. Cut out the patterns through the paper and the stencil cards, using a sharp hobby knife or scalpel. It is easier to cut curves if you move the card to meet the blade rather than the other way around.

4 Plan the position of your daisies on the wall, carefully measuring the distances between them and marking the wall with a pencil as a guide. You will need to draw a basic grid of squares to ensure accurate placement and lining-up of the daisies. In order to draw straight vertical lines, use a plumb line made of string, with bluetack to secure it at the top and a key tied to the end of the string as the weight.

5   To complete your pencil grid on the wall, use a rule together with a spirit level to draw accurate horizontal lines. Keep measuring carefully as you draw the lines, to ensure that your squares are not only straight but also the same size and distance apart from one another. The squares need to match the size of your stencil card for accurate positioning. Next, spray the back of the stencils lightly with spray mount and leave for five minutes until they become tacky.

6   Squeeze out your selected acrylic or other water-based paints onto a clean, dry plate. Begin loading the stencil brush, just covering the ends of all the bristles, then dab most of the paint off onto absorbent kitchen paper, so that the brush is almost dry. Don't overload the brush.

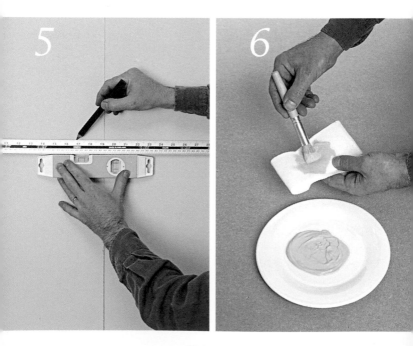

7 Starting with the petal stencil, carefully place it over one of the marked squares, just allowing the tacky adhesive to hold it in position, and begin dabbing the paint onto the wall. Apply the paint by wiping the brush over the cutout in the stencil card, beginning at the edges and then filling in toward the center of the petal. For a three-dimensional effect, add more paint to some areas of the petals to darken them.

8 Allow the petal stencils to dry (because the paint is applied so sparingly, this will not take long), then take up your second stencil card, again sticking it gently in place, and use a contrasting color to stencil the centers. When all the paint is dry, carefully remove the card. Repeat until you have stencilled the required area.

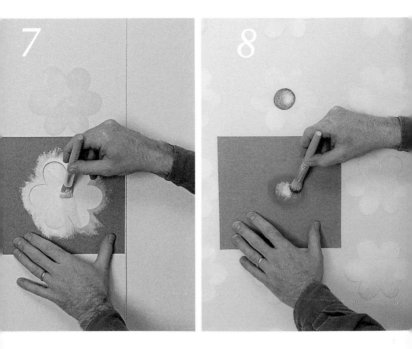

15

making a
shelf with peg rail

A peg rail is always useful in a child's bedroom—there is generally enough mess around without having anywhere to hang robes and coats. Combine the peg rail with a handy shelf, as in this project, and you immediately have an item that is twice as useful. This unit is relatively quick and easy to assemble, requiring no special skills or materials, and will prove an invaluable and attractive addition to any children's room.

Materials (all lumber is softwood unless otherwise stated)

Pegrail board: 1 piece of 8 x 1 x 36 in. lumber

Shelf: 1 piece of 2 x 1 x 36 in. lumber

Shelf edging: 1 piece of 2 x ½ x 60 in. lumber

Pegs: 5 pieces of ¾ x 1 x 5 in. lumber

1 small tin of matte varnish • 1 small tin of acrylic paint • 2 paint brushes

Tools

Workbench • 2 G-clamps • Hand saw • Miter saw • Hammer • Panel pins • Wood glue • Nail punch • Abrasive paper and sanding block • Wood filler

Skill level

Beginner

Time

4 hours

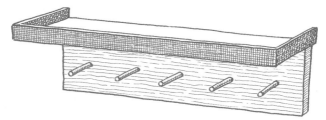

1 Measure and cut the peg rail board and shelf pieces to the dimensions given in the list of materials, using a workbench and clamps to secure the wood as necessary. Sand off and smooth any rough edges or splinters from your saw cuts.

2 For the shelf edging, take the piece of 2 x ½ in. timber and measure out a complete shelf surround from it, to the same dimensions as those of the shelf. Use a miter saw to cut mitered corners for the shelf surround at a 45-degree angle. Again, sand and smooth off any uneven areas of the saw cuts.

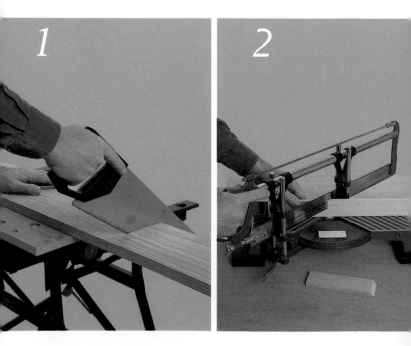

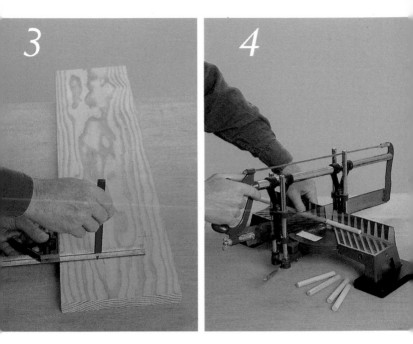

3 Work out how many pegs you would like to include with your shelf (in the illustrated example on page 17 it is five, but it could be more or fewer). Using a pencil, rule, and set square, measure and mark the position of the holes that the pegs will fit into on the peg rail board. Ensure that the holes are evenly spaced along the length of the peg rail board and that the end pegs will not be positioned too closely to the ends of the board.

4 Cut the required number of 4 x 3 in. pegs from ¾ in. dowel, using the miter saw. Ensure that the cuts are straight and that the pegs are all exactly the same length. Smooth off any rough edges with abrasive paper.

5 Using the marks you made in step 3 for guidance, drill ¾ in. holes on the peg rail board. Make sure you pre-set your drill-bit to a ½-in. depth that will ensure you do not break through the back of the peg rail board while you are drilling. Also drill three evenly spaced holes across the top third of the peg rail board (that is, above the peg holes), this time drilling all the way through the board. These holes will take the screws required to fix the peg rail board to the wall.

6 Drill five evenly spaced clearance holes along the top side of the shelf, through which you will fix the shelf to the peg rail board.

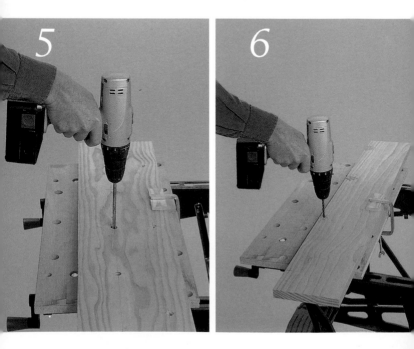

7 Replace your drill-bit with a countersinking bit and carefully countersink the holes that you have just drilled. This will ensure that the screw heads do not protrude from the surface of the shelf.

8 Secure the peg rail board in the clamps of your workbench with the uppermost edge facing up toward you. Place the back side of the shelf over the edge of the peg rail board at the position where they will be joined. Drill pilot holes into the top edge of the peg rail board, through the countersunk clearance holes that you drilled into the shelf in step 6.

9   Glue and pin the shelf edging all the way around the shelf. Hammer six panel pins in, each 6 in. apart, along the length of the shelf edge. Use two panel pins to attach the edging at each end. The shelf surround should be positioned so that its bottom aligns with the bottom of the shelf, its top edge sitting up to create a retaining "lip" around the entire shelf.

10 Carefully punch the protruding pin heads into the shelf surround using a nail punch and hammer.

Helpful hints

Never use too much glue when woodworking. When making a joint, spread only a thin layer over one surface and immediately wipe away any excess with a damp cloth.

11 Apply a thin line of glue to one of the two joining edges of the shelf and the peg rail board. Be careful not to use too much glue, as otherwise it will squeeze out of the joint and over the wood when the shelf and board are put together. Carefully screw the shelf and peg rail board together, through the pilot holes that you drilled in steps 6 and 8.

12 Finally, position each of the pegs in the holes on the peg rail board, using a spot of wood glue to secure each one. Sand and fill the peg rail board and shelf as necessary and paint or varnish to your taste.

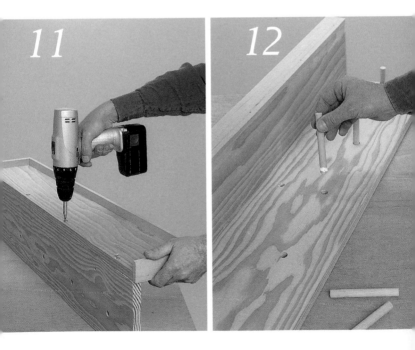

making picket
window shutters

These picket-style window shutters make an attractive and refreshing alternative to the standard drapes or blinds that currently adorn your child's bedroom window. Their sturdy construction means they are strong and child-proof, but they look stylish and let in plenty of light. It is important to ensure symmetry throughout the design and accuracy with all the joints, but so long as you have basic carpentry skills, the shutters should not prove too difficult to make. The number of pickets required will vary according to the width of your window.

Materials (all lumber is softwood unless otherwise stated)

Shutter slats: 10 pieces of lumber ½ x 3 x 36 in. (calculate number to fit window)

Cross braces: 2 pieces of lumber 2 x 1 x 36 in.

Upright battens: 2 pieces of lumber 2 x 2 x 28 in.

4 black iron hinges • 1 black iron cabin hook and eye • No. 6 (1½ in.) screws • Panel pins • Wall plugs • Wood glue • Wood filler

Tools

Workbench • 2 G-clamps • Power drill with screw, countersinking, and ⅛ in. bits • Set-square • Hand saw • Miter saw • Hammer • Nail punch • Abrasive paper

Skill level

Advanced

Time

8 hours

1 The number of slats you require to make your wooden
shutters will depend on the size of your window. Each
shutter must be the same size with the same number
of slats. Carefully measure the width and height of the
window before you begin work. Then, cut all the pieces
of wood to the longest length that will be required—
that of the two center slats. Each of these should
measure 3 in. less in length than your window reveal.
Then lay out the timber for one shutter on a workbench,
putting a piece of scrap wood underneath.

2 Mark the top center of the longest piece of wood (one
of the center slats). Measure 12 in. down the side from
the top of the first piece on the other side, mark the
center, and then draw a diagonal line to connect the
two marks.

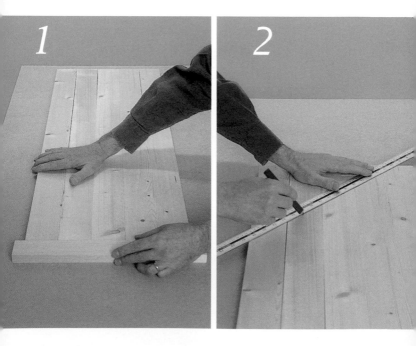

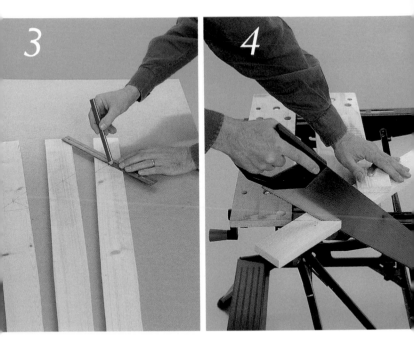

3 Mark the center point of each slat where the line crosses them all. Use a rule and/or combination square to mark out a 45-degree peak on each slat. These will be cut out as the points of the slats. Hold the wood firmly on the workbench as you do this, to keep the slats still as you mark them with the pencil.

4 Cut the peaks as marked out using a saw. You may find it easier to clamp the slats to a workbench as you do this, but be sure to protect their surfaces if you do so. Repeat steps 1–4 for the set of slats needed to make the second shutter.

5 Clamp each slat in turn in a workbench and then smooth off all the sharp edges, using a sanding block or abrasive paper.

6 Butt the slats together using scrap wood at their ends to help line them up correctly. Ensure that all the slats for both shutters are evenly aligned across the bottom. Once you are satisfied that the base line for both shutters is straight, draw a line across all ten slats 3 in. up from the base line and 3 in. down from the top of the shortest side. These lines mark where the wooden cross braces will attach to all the slats. Place the lower cross brace with its bottom edge on the bottom line and the upper brace with its top edge on the upper line. Draw along the edges of both cross braces.

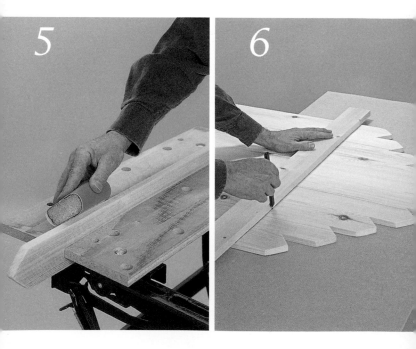

7 Lay the two cross brace pieces on the work surface.
Place all the slats for both shutters on top of them,
positioning the cross braces correctly along the pencil
lines you drew in step 6. Use a set-square to ensure
that each slat is correctly aligned across the cross
braces. Mark and drill pilot screw holes in all the slats
to attach them to the cross braces. Each slat will
require fixing to each of the cross braces with two
evenly spaced screws, top and bottom.

8 To space out the slats evenly across the cross braces,
wedge a spare slat sideways in between each pair of
the pieces. Attach the first slat with two screws in each
of the cross braces, top and bottom. As you fix the
slats, constantly use a set-square to check that they are
all perfectly square to the cross braces.

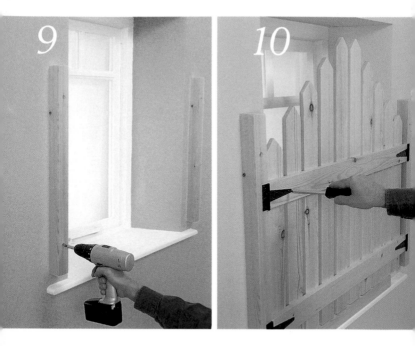

9 Measure the width of both shutters butted together to determine accurate sitings for the wall battens. Mark the positions for the batten fixing points on the wall in pencil then drill, countersink, and secure the battens, using wallplugs to receive the screws. Be sure not to site the fixing screws where they might impede the ideal positioning of the shutters' hinges.

10 Mark and drill pilot holes into both the battens and the cross braces for fixing the hinges. Attach the hinges with No. 6 (1½ in.) screws, pushing them down as you fix them to the cross braces to minimize the "play" in the hinges and prevent the shutters dropping at all when they have been separated. Use a piece of 2 x 2 in. wood to support the shutters from beneath as you secure the hinges to them, as shown.

11 Using a set-square and pencil, draw a line to the center of each of the back braces and saw through them carefully, doing the top one first. Keep the shutters braced with the piece of timber beneath them.

12 When you have sawn through both back braces, sand off the cut edges to smooth them and ease the contact point of the two shutters. Finally, attach a cabin hook with which to close the shutters.

Helpful hints

Check to see that your wall is square before attaching the fixing battens and shutters. It is essential that everything lines up, or the shutters will not open and close properly.

block-printing a **roller blind**

It is easy to brighten your children's room by buying lots of decorative fixtures, but far more fulfilling to make your own. This innovative project involves taking a plain, standard roller blind and transforming it in no time at all into something special for the window of your child's room. Color-stamping with foam die-cuts is a cheap and effective way of transforming not only window blinds but just about any other piece of fabric, wooden furniture, and bare walls. The technique is simple to learn, and quick and inexpensive to put into effect.

Materials
Roller blind (dimensions to fit your own window)—pale blue • Dense foam—camping mat or similar type thick card (shoe box lid or other scrap) • Newspapers • Dark blue, yellow, and white acrylic paint

Tools
Tape measure • Scalpel/hobby knife and spare blades • Low-tack spray adhesive • Small white dinner plate • 3 small foam rollers—children's craft type

Skill level
Intermediate

Time
4 hours

1 Measure the width of the window. Cut the blind to fit. Then, measure the width of the roller blind to calculate the number and size of squares that will fit evenly. For example, a 36-in. width equates to nine squares measuring 4 in. each.

2 Trace the sun and moon designs from page 108 of this book onto paper and enlarge them to the required size on a photocopier. The designs both need to fit comfortably into the squares. Cut out two squares of paper to the required size and draw one design on each. Place the squares over the sheet of foam and cut out foam blocks to the same dimensions as the squares.

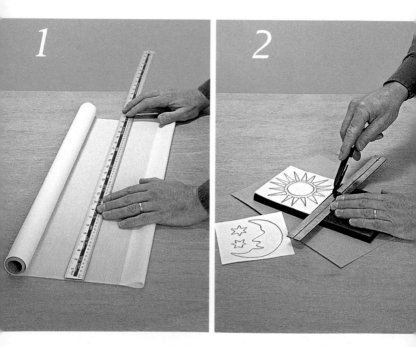

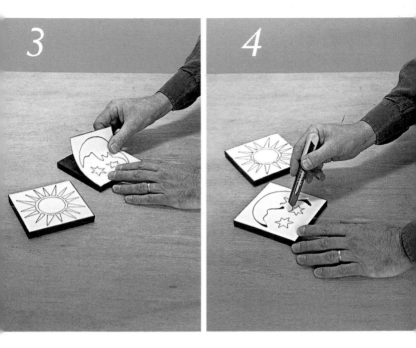

3 When you are satisfied that the cut blocks of foam precisely match the squares holding the sun and moon designs, apply low-tack spray adhesive to the back of the patterns and stick them onto the blocks of foam. Follow the manufacturer's instructions and make sure that a window is open for ventilation.

4 Use a sharp hobby knife or scalpel to cut around the outlines of the pattern shapes into the foam blocks to the depth of ¼ in. Make the cuts as evenly and cleanly as possible, ensuring that you do not press through to the bottom of the foam block. Cut off any extraneous pieces that obstruct a clean line.

35

5 Once you have cleanly cut around the sun and moon designs, remove the paper templates and bend the foam blocks to open up the cut lines that you have made. Carefully use the hobby knife to cut away the extraneous foam around the designs, leaving the designs raised in clear relief ¼ in. above the remaining bottom of the foam blocks.

6 Cut out a square of card to the same dimensions as the foam blocks. This will be used as a positional guide and spacer when stamping the background. Then, cut out a plain block of foam to the same size, for applying the blue checkerboard pattern prior to stamping on the sun and moon designs.

7 Use short strips of masking tape to affix little handles to the backs of each of the foam blocks. Make raised tape "loops" with which you can hold the foam blocks steady from behind. This will make it easier to stamp the blind later on.

8 Squeeze dark blue acrylic paint onto a clean, dry, ceramic plate and run the foam roller through it until it is evenly coated with paint all over. Then, run the roller over the plain foam square that you cut out in step 6. Ensure that the whole face of the foam square is evenly coated with paint.

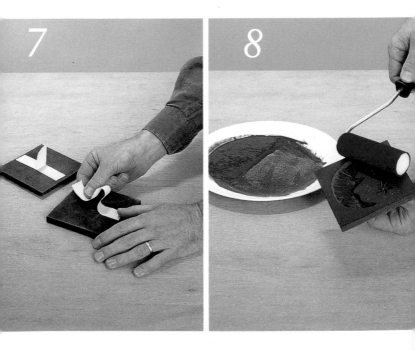

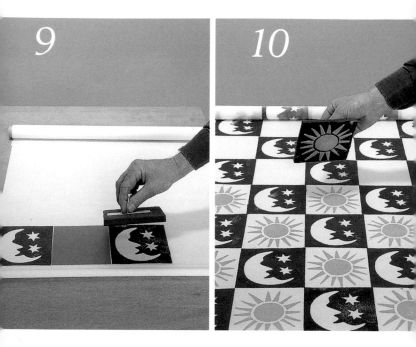

9 Unfurl the roller blind on a piece of scrap plyboard or an old tabletop. Begin stamping the dark blue checkerboard pattern in one of the bottom corners of the blind, just above the seam containing the wooden slat at its end. Use the card square that you cut out in step 6 as a spacer alongside each stamped dark blue square to ascertain the position for the next one. When the dark blue paint squares have all dried thoroughly, squeeze white paint onto a plate and use a fresh roller to stamp the moon motif centrally in each of them.

10 When you have stamped all the alternate dark blue squares and white moon motifs so that the checkerboard pattern and moon effect is complete, squeeze yellow acrylic paint onto a clean plate and use a fresh roller to coat the sun design foam block. Stamp a sun motif centrally in each of the unpainted squares.

11 Ascertain the width of the roller blind once more and mark the positions for its fixing brackets in pencil on the window frame. If necessary, drill pilot holes for the bracket screws into the window frame, and then fix the roller brackets in place. Use a standard, non-electric screwdriver to reduce the likelihood of causing damage to the decor of the window frame.

12 Finally, roll up and pre-tension your roller blind as necessary, in accordance with the manufacturer's instructions. Secure the blind in the brackets and pull it down to enjoy the full effect of your sun and moon design.

making an **underbed drawer**

Storage is a constant problem in children's rooms. The key to making the most of your child's personal space is maximizing the square-footage available. There are few more space-efficient solutions than this brightly decorated, stylish underbed storage drawer. Made out of inexpensive lumber and board, and mounted on castors, this drawer is simple to make, capacious, and easy to use. It can be personalized with your child's favorite colors or characters and will supply a long-term solution to bedtime storage problems.

Materials (all lumber is softwood unless otherwise stated)

Bottom: 1 piece of MDF ¾ x 30 x 48 in.
Front: 1 piece of MDF ¾ x 8 x 48 in.
Back: 1 piece of MDF ¾ x 8 x 48 in.
Sides: 2 pieces of MDF ¾ x 8 x 30 in.
Paper pattern • Wood glue • No. 6 (1½ in.) screws • 4 x 2½ in.-deep castors • Paint—2 contrasting colors of gloss paint and one undercoat • White spirit

Tools

Workbench • Clamps • Jigsaw • Set-square • Drill fitted with 1¼ in., ⅛ in., screw, and countersinking bits • Tape measure • Carpenter's pencil • Abrasive paper/sanding block • Paint brush

Skill level

Intermediate

Time

4 hours

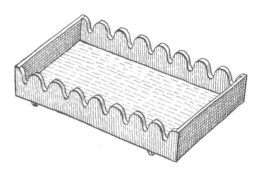

1 Begin by cutting the five pieces that make up the drawer to the measurements given in the list of materials. Once you have made all the cuts, smooth off any rough edges with abrasive paper.

2 Draw a straight line along the length of one of the side pieces, 2 in. in from the longest edge. Using a compass and pencil, mark evenly spaced points 3¼ in. apart. These are the places that holes will be drilled in the first stage of creating the curved edging pattern.

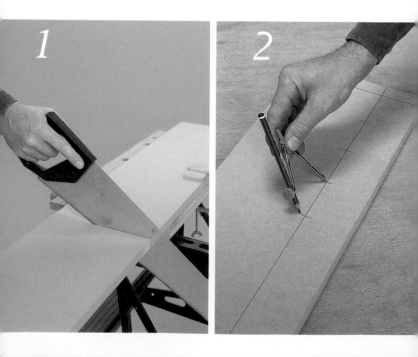

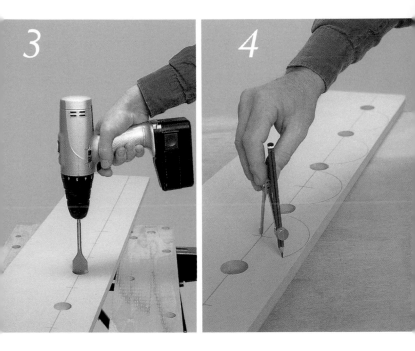

3 Clamp the side piece to a workbench and use a drill fitted with a 1¼ in. drill-bit to drill holes at each of the points marked in step 2.

4 Again using the compass and pencil, position the point of the compass at the precise mid-point between each of the drilled holes. Draw semi-circles from one drilled hole to another, so that the outer edge of the semi-circle meets the edge of the wood. This is the pattern for the decorative front top edge of the storage box.

5 With the front piece still clamped firmly onto a workbench, use the jigsaw to begin cutting the decorative edge. When cutting the curves, work at an even, steady pace, moving the saw with your whole arm and shoulder and not just from the wrist. Take your time, ensuring that you follow the pencil lines closely so that the curves will be as consistent as possible.

6 When you have cut out the curves along the entire length of the front piece, sand all the edges smooth. Use a piece of abrasive paper wrapped around a bit of scrap dowel to get well into the narrow bottom of each cut.

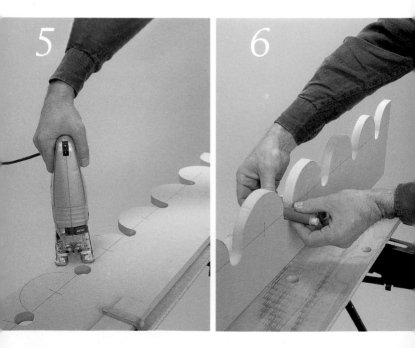

7 Mark, drill, and then countersink evenly spaced fixing holes across the bottom of the front of the side piece, in order for it to be fitted to the base of the storage box.

8 Take one of the two shorter end pieces and drill five evenly spaced pilot holes along the bottom edge. Glue along one end of the bottom piece, line up the end piece and screw the bottom and the end piece together through the pilot holes that you have just drilled. Repeat on the other side.

Helpful hints

You will generally find it easier to clamp wood to a workbench when you are drilling or cutting it with a jigsaw. Alternatively, ask someone to help you hold the wood.

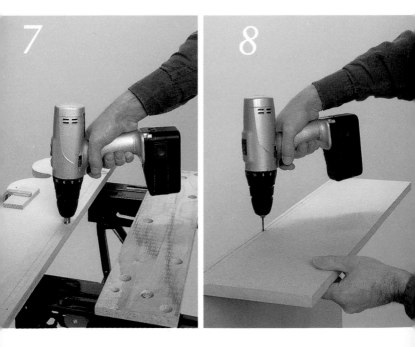

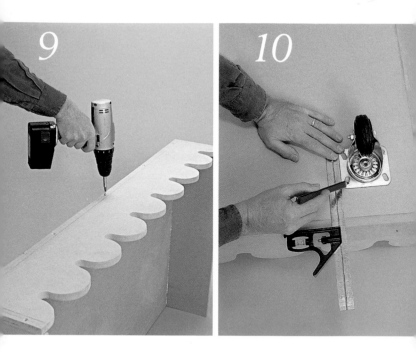

9 Use the same method to fit the front piece onto the base and to join it and the back piece onto the upright ends of the drawer. Ensure that the joints of the drawer are all fully squared-up and even, and that your screws locate neatly in the pre-drilled pilot holes. Thoroughly wipe away any excess glue along the joints with a clean, damp cloth.

10 Once it is complete, turn the box over and mark the positions for the castors at each of its four corners. Use a set-square and pencil to ensure that each castor will be accurately positioned in the same place at each corner of the drawer.

11 Drill pilot holes for the screws to attach the castors, being careful not to drill through the entire thickness of the base of the box. Follow the manufacturer's instructions to fix the castors onto the base.

12 Sand the box as necessary, paying particular attention to all the joints of the five pieces. Use a filling knife and a proprietary wood filler to fill all the screw holes and then sand these off smoothly when the filler has dried thoroughly. Decorate the entire box a bright primary color, in gloss or matte paint according to your preference.

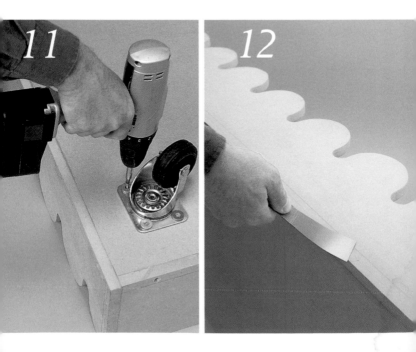

building a
desk and shelf unit

Every child wants to draw pictures or practice their letters once they can pick up a crayon. This desk and shelf unit provides the personal space they need. It is easy to build and space-efficient in its design, fitting neatly into any available alcove, recess, or awkward corner of a child's bedroom. Ensure that all your joints are square and your angles are in line with your walls as you build, and aim for a good, tight, fit for the main desktop of the unit. If you prefer, paint the entire unit for a long-lasting, hard-wearing finish.

Materials (all lumber is softwood unless otherwise stated)

Desktop: 1 piece of MDF 1 x 24 in. x (width of alcove + 4 in.)
Shelf: 1 piece of MDF ¾ x 8 in. x (width of alcove)
Shelf supports: 2 pieces of MDF ¾ x 6 x 10 in.
Desk leg: 1 piece of PAR timber 2 x 2 x 27 in.
Desk edging: 1 piece of PAR timber 2 x 1 in. x 6 ft.
• Wall plugs • Screws • Wood glue • Panel pins • Wood filler •
Primer • Paint

Tools

Workbench • Hand saw • Miter saw • Power drill • Screwdriver bit • Hammer • Set-square • Bradawl • Spirit level • Straightedge • Tape measure

Skill level

Advanced

Time

8 hours

1 Select a recess or alcove in your child's bedroom and measure its width. Using a spirit level and pencil, draw a line on the wall 28 in. above the floor. (Check that this height is suitable for your child and amend accordingly.) This line marks the height of the desktop you are going to build. Ensure that the line is straight across the entire width of the alcove, checking for any anomalies in the evenness of the wall as you draw the line.

2 Measure and cut three 2 x 1 in. battens, one for the back and two for the side walls of the recess to make the frame of the desk. Mark evenly spaced fixing holes on each batten and drill them through with a ⅛ in. drill bit. Attach a batten to the back wall first, marking fixing holes on the wall with a bradawl through the pilot holes in the batten.

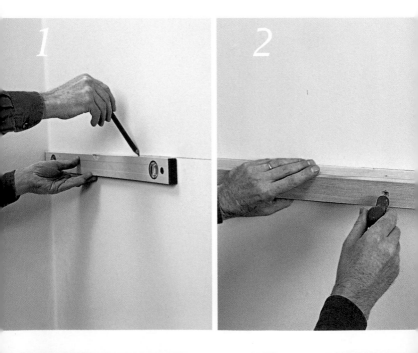

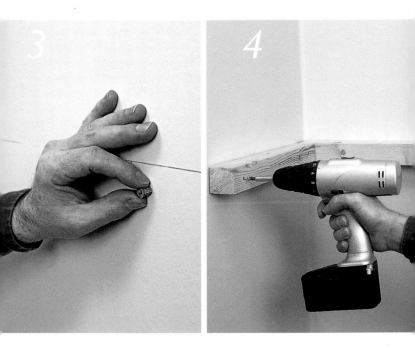

3 Drill holes into the wall for attaching the batten, and press in wall plugs for receiving the screws. Use cavity/plasterboard plugs in partition or hollow walls, to ensure that the battens will be securely fastened and will be able to take the weight of the desk and shelf unit.

4 Drill pilot holes through the undersides of the side battens before fixing them to the walls, in order to attach the MDF top later on. Then, mark screw holes to attach the side battens to the wall, drill and fix them so that they both align perfectly with the batten that you have already mounted on the back wall.

5 Measure and cut out the desktop from the 1 in. MDF board. The desktop measurements should correspond precisely with the dimensions of the alcove to ensure a snug fit. Carefully check the fit of the desktop and its correct alignment over the battens.

6 Cut the leg to fit. Place it in position. Check the evenness of the desktop with a spirit level and adjust the height of the leg as necessary. This should be the height from floor level to the top of the side-wall batten. Mark and drill four pilot holes, and then screw the MDF desktop firmly to the leg.

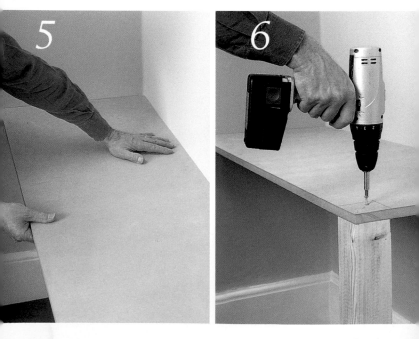

7 Attach the MDF desktop to the wall battens, by
screwing through the pilot holes that you drilled in the
battens earlier. Make sure you get a good, even contact
between the screws through the undersides of the
battens and the desktop. It might be a good idea to get
someone to put their weight on the desktop as you
attach it to the battens.

8 Take two pieces of desk edging, cut to your
requirements, and miter the two ends that will meet
at the corner of the exposed edges. In the example
illustrated on page 51, that is the front edge and the
right-hand side that extends from the alcove. Glue and
pin the edging in place, ensuring that the joints fit
neatly together.

9 Position and mark the shelf supports and drill pilot holes through the top of the MDF desktop. Then fix the shelf supports to the desktop from underneath.

10 Position the shelf on the shelf supports and use a set-square to ensure that the supports are perfectly square to the shelf prior to fixing. Draw pencil guidelines and two evenly spaced fixing hole marks for each support.

Helpful hints

There is no "tolerance" in MDF, so it is vital to drill pilot holes accurately into it. Always ensure that the positions of all screw holes line up properly before using your drill.

11 Drill pilot holes through the MDF shelf at the marks you made with the set-square and pencil. Countersink the screw holes and then fix the shelf to the shelf supports, ensuring that the screws line up with the pilot holes and the shelf fits squarely to the supports and is flush with the back wall.

12 Measure and cut the shelf edging, mitering the corners at the exposed ends. Glue and pin the edging with the bottom edge flush to the bottom of the shelf, so that the edging sits up as a retaining "lip." Fill any gaps with proprietary wood filler and sand the unit as necessary, paying particular attention to all the joints, and then paint or varnish as you wish.

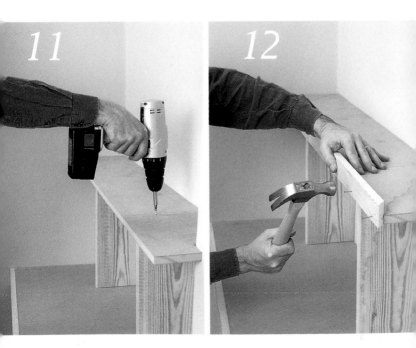

making a
wooden toybox

Storage is always a problem in children's rooms, particularly if you are short of space. This attractive decorated wooden toybox can help, and will look good at the foot of any bed or tucked away in a convenient corner.

Materials (all lumber is softwood unless otherwise stated)

Lid (top): 1 piece of MDF ½ x 10¼ x 26¼ in. (N.B. Ensure that the dimensions of the box-lid are ¼ in. greater than the box itself)

Lid (sides): 2 pieces of 1 x 2 x 10¼ in. PAR; 2 pieces of 1 x 2 x 26¼ in. PAR

Lid (surround): 2 pieces of ¾ x 3 x 10¼ in. PAR; 2 pieces of ¾ x 3 x 26¼ in. PAR

Base: 1 piece of MDF ½ x 10 x 26 in.

Front and back: 2 pieces of PAR 1 x 8 x 26 in.

Ends: 2 pieces of PAR 1 x 8 x 8 in.

Plinth: 2 pieces of ¾ x 3 x 10 in. PAR; 2 pieces of ¾ x 3 x 26 in. PAR

Backstop: 1 piece of PAR 1½ x 1½ x 20 in.

Wood glue • Screws • 2 x 3-in. hinges • Wood filler • 2 x paint colors for box and lid • 3 tubes of acrylic paint for ABC on lid top

Tools

Workbench • Power drill, with ⅛ in., screwdriver, and countersinking bits • Handsaw • Miter saw • Clamps • Bradawl • Abrasive paper • Transfer paper • Paintbrush fine/medium • Artist's brush • Pencil

Skill level

Advanced

Time

8 hours

1 Once you have cut out all the pieces to the required dimensions, use a pencil to mark the fixing positions of both ends of the box to the base, front, and back. Set the pieces of wood against one another, edge to edge, ensuring that the proposed joints are fully squared-up and even before you draw pencil lines along the edges of the end pieces.

2 Drill screw holes in the ends of the box and then line up the front and back pieces and drill pilot holes into them through the holes you have just drilled in the ends. Ensure that the ends are square to the front and back before you drill the pilot holes. Repeat on all four corners. You may find it easier to clamp the end in the workbench and drill the holes from above.

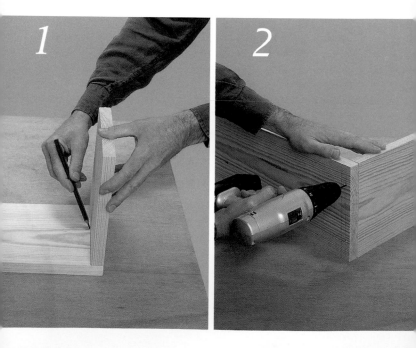

3 Countersink the drilled holes on both the front and back
of the box. This will ensure that the screwheads are
fully recessed later on, avoiding any sharp edges for a
child to catch themselves upon.

4 Glue and then screw the front, back, and ends of the
box together. Do not use too much wood glue. If you
do it will squeeze out over the surfaces as the joints are
put together. Take extra care to keep all joints square.

Helpful hints

*Good joints are the key to success with most woodworking.
Take your time in lining-up and fixing your joints, and ask
someone to help if you need another pair of hands.*

5 Fix the base piece to the box, using the same method as described in steps 2–4. Once again, be careful not to use too much glue and ensure that all joints are straight and corners match up evenly. Repeat steps 1–5 for the sides of the lid.

6 This wooden toybox features a plinth around its bottom and an overlapping surround on the edge of its lid. Cut the surround pieces to a little longer than the length of the sides and ends of the box/lid, and then mark the positions of the mitered joints for the surrounds, using a pencil. In each case, clearly mark the direction of the cut against the corners of each of the outer frame lid pieces and plinth pieces.

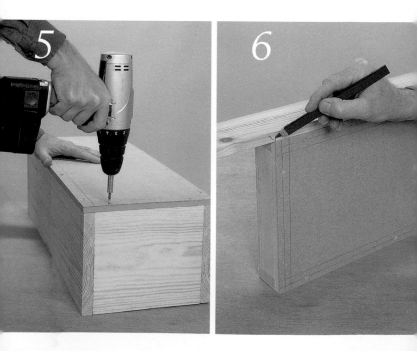

7 Cut each of the miter joints using a mitering saw, making sure you follow the line of the cut marked in pencil on the surround and plinth pieces. Ensure that the angle of the cut is precisely the same for each miter, to guarantee good, tight joints.

8 Once the miters have all been cut to fit correctly, glue the surround pieces to the lid of the box and the plinth to its base. Then secure both surrounds additionally with pins. You will find it easier to hammer the pins most of the way through the plinth and lid surround pieces before gluing them to the box.

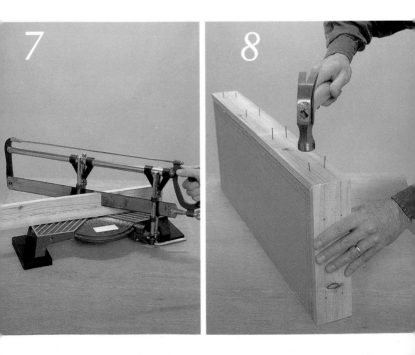

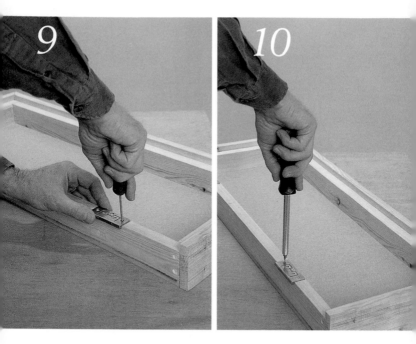

9 Measure 4 in. or so in from each end of the box lid, along the back edge. Position one of the lid hinges at this point, folded closed and flush to the edge. Use a bradawl to mark the positions of the holes for the hinge screws, on both the edge of the box and on the lid. Repeat with the other hinge. Take trouble to ensure that the hinges line up correctly and allow a good fit between the lid and the box before you mark the screw holes with the bradawl.

10 Drill pilot holes for the hinge-screws in the lid using a ⅛-in. drill bit. Then, fix the hinges with the screws attaching the outer part of the hinge to the lid.

11 Screw the lid hinges on to the back edge of the box. You might find it easier to support the lid on a block of wood or have someone hold it for you as you screw the hinges onto the box.

12 Cut the backstop to fit just beyond the width of the box hinges on each side. Cut decorative miters on the ends of the backstop. Center and position the backstop just below the hinges and draw around it to mark its position on the back of the box. Mark and drill pilot holes for the screws to attach the backstop to the box.

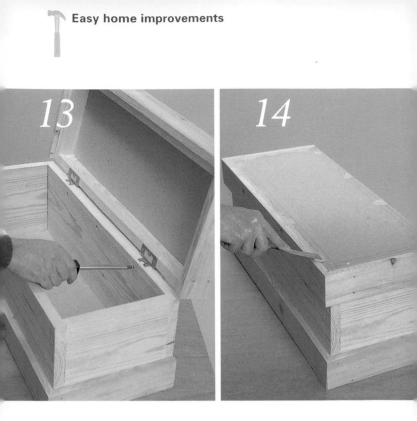

13 Attach the backstop to the back of the box by screwing into it through the drilled pilot holes from inside the box. Ask someone to hold the backstop in place as you screw into it.

14 Use wood filler and apply with a small filling knife or spatula to fill all the screw holes. Once the filler has set, sand it down to a smooth finish.

Helpful hints

Don't worry if you make a mistake with a joint or the positioning of a screw hole. Most minor errors can be rectified with a good wood filler and careful sanding.

15 Paint the lid and the plinth of the box in red and the rest of the base in yellow, for contrast. Write "ABC"—or maybe your child's name—onto a piece of tracing paper and attach it to the top of the box over a piece of transfer paper of the same size. (N.B. Place the *chalky* side down against the top of the box.) Write over the "ABC" outline as shown, using a hard pencil, so that the transfer letters adhere to the top of the box.

16 Once the outlines of the letters are transferred onto the top of the box through the transfer paper, fill the letters in using a different colored paint for each one.

making an
oven play-cupboard

Lots of children like to play "house" as they are growing up, and there are few better props you could give them than this colorful and fun oven play cupboard. The project requires time and care, but with basic carpentry skills and a little precision you will get a good result. The unit is not only fun to play with but also provides useful storage space for the more cluttered children's room.

Materials

Back: 1 piece of MDF ¾ x 16 x 24 in.

Front: 1 piece of MDF ¾ x 16 x 24 in.

Sides: 2 pieces of MDF ¾ x 16 x 24 in.

Top: 1 piece of MDF ¾ x 14½ x 14½ in.

Base: 1 piece of MDF ¾ x 14½ x 14½ in.

Door: 1 piece of MDF ¾ x 14 x 20 in.

Shelf: 1 piece of MDF ¾ x 14 x 14 in.

Hob surround: 4 pieces of MDF ¾ x 3 x 17 in.

Clear Perspex 12 x 16 in. • Two hinges • Screws • Stencil card • Clear varnish • Paint (main color plus small tin of black enamel)

Tools

Workbench • Drill • Screwdriver bits • Wood glue • Jigsaw • Hand saw • Panel pins • Wood filler • Abrasive paper • Paint brush • Stencil brush • Scalpel • Brush

Skill level

Advanced

Time

8 hours

1 Measure and cut all the pieces to the dimensions given in the list of materials. Hold up the edges of the different pieces to one another on the workbench and then draw fixing guidelines on their edges to the thickness of the boards. Mark evenly spaced, screw-fixing positions on the sides, top, shelf, base, and back of the play cupboard, using a rule and a pencil. You will need five screw holes along each vertical edge and three along the horizontals.

2 Drill pilot holes for all screw fixings in all the main pieces that make up the play cupboard and countersink them in order to recess the screw-heads.

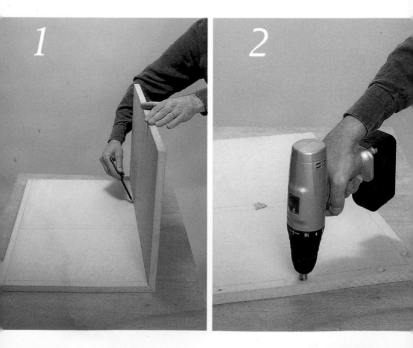

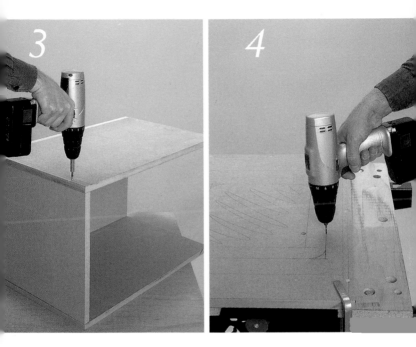

3 Glue and then screw one of the sides to the back of the unit and then attach the base with screws only. Apply only a thin layer of glue, and do not use it at all for the sides-to-base fixings, to avoid glue spreading over the inside of the base. Attach the other side to the base and the back. Finally, fix the shelf in place.

4 Mark out the oven door outline on the front board in pencil using the circular base of a can or saucer to create the characteristic rounded corners of the oven door. Mark out the oven door window area. Drill a ½-in. hole on the edge of the oven window area you are going to cut out, to allow you to insert the jigsaw blade. Then, drill three small holes in a row in the position where the hinges will go until you have a hole large enough to slip the jigsaw blade into (about ½ in. in diameter), to cut out the door area.

5 Insert the jigsaw blade into the ½ in. hole on the edge of the cooker window that you are going to cut out. Cut carefully around the pencil outline until the window is fully cut out. Then, insert the jigsaw into the smaller hole next to where the hinges will be fixed and cut carefully around the outer outline. Be careful not to cut into your workbench. Sand down any rough areas or splinters caused by your cutting.

6 Attach the front frame of the cooker to the sides, base, and top of the unit using 1½ in. No. 6 screws through the ¾ in. MDF board.

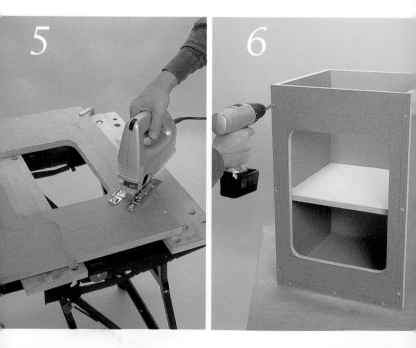

7 For the oven window, cut a piece of Perspex to size (12 in. x 16 in.), by scoring with a hobby knife several times and snapping the cut line over a straight edge. Mark and drill screw holes at each corner and in the middle of each side of the Perspex in order to fit it to the back of the oven door.

8 Drill pilot holes into the door through each of the holes drilled in the Perspex, to the dimension of the shank of the No. 4 screws you will use to affix the Perspex to the door. Use brass screw cups to recess the header of the screws as you attach the Perspex to the door.

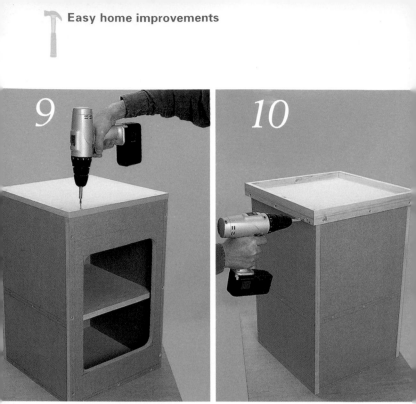

9   Attach the top of the oven to the unit using glue and 1½ in. No. 6 screws into countersunk pilot holes.

10   Mark and cut edging pieces to the width of the unit for all four sides at the top of the oven, cutting 45-degree miter joints at their corners. Smooth off any splinters and rough edges with fine abrasive paper. Drill and countersink pilot holes in the edging pieces and unit sides in order to fix the edging pieces to the unit with screws. When fixing the edging pieces, set them so that their bottom edges align with the bottom edge of the unit's top. The tops of the edging pieces will then sit up about 1 in. above the top of the unit. Ensure that you drill and screw the edging pieces well away from the screws already holding the unit together.

11 Mark and fix the hinges to the oven door with ¾ in. No.4 screws. Then offer the oven door up to the unit, position it correctly with the Perspex fittings inside the oven and mark the hinge screw holes on the unit edge. Drill pilot holes and then attach the hinged oven door with No. 4 screws.

12 Line up the handle above the front of the shelf and mark the screw-hole positions on the inside of the oven door. Drill pilot holes to the width of a No. 4 screw shank. Fix the handle to the oven door with screws. Use a screwdriver and No. 4 screws to attach a magnet catch to the inside of the door and the front of the unit.

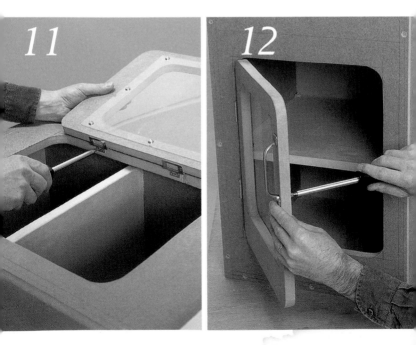

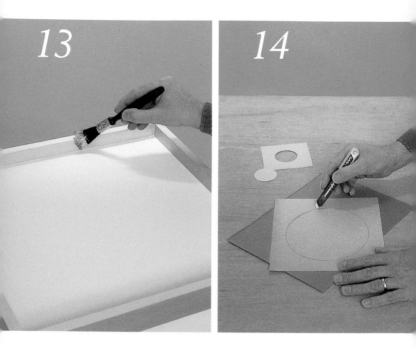

13 Paint the entire unit in cream, finishing off the top surround in gray for added authenticity.

14 Using a scalpel and card, cut out two circular stencils—a large one for painting on the hot plates and a smaller one for the cooker control knobs.

Helpful hints

Whenever painting with stencils, always move the brush from the edge of the stencil cut inwards—that is, paint from "out-to-in"—to avoid paint getting under the edge.

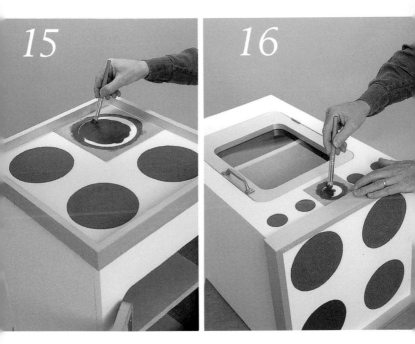

15 Paint three of the hot plates in gray, dragging the paint across the circle from the outside to the center, to prevent the paint from creeping under the edge of the stencil. Once your stencil card has dried off, paint the fourth and last stencil in red, so this hotplate looks as if it is "on."

16 Finally, use the smaller stencil to paint on the oven knobs in gray, again, painting across the stencil from the outside in, to avoid paint getting under the edges of the stencil and smudging on the unit. Paint the middle knob in red, to represent the oven switch.

Accessories & toys

making an appliqué-
cat bed cover

Children love personalized clothing and soft accessories. This cozy and colorful bed quilt will delight them and give the decor of their bedroom a boost at the same time. The quilt is not difficult to make, although an electric sewing machine will save you a lot of time. The fleece fabric at the heart of the item is warm, versatile, and surprisingly inexpensive. It looks great adorned with the red and white gingham cloth and the double cat design will brighten up any child's bedtime. Pre-select your own fabric colors, cat features, and details to ensure a truly personal design.

Materials

36 x 52 in. gingham fabric, 44 in. width x 1.5 yd. • 1.6 x 1.5 yd. polar fleece (60 in. width x 2 yd.) • 36 x 52 in. quilter's wadding (60 in. width x 1.5 yd.) • 20 in. iron-on wadding (18 in. square) • Contrasting tapestry wool in 2 colors • White sewing thread

Tools

Pins • Scissors • Broad needle for embroidery stitching • Fine needle for tacking • Steam iron • Electric sewing machine

Skill level

Intermediate

Time

4 hours

Easy home improvements

1. Photocopy the cat pattern template on page 108 onto a sheet of paper up to 17 x 22 in. in size. The cat pattern needs to fit into a 13½ x 11 in. rectangular transfer onto two sheets of tissue paper. Carefully trace the design onto tracing paper, using a black pen for the outline.

2. Use a rule and scissors to measure and cut out two 16 x 14 in. rectangles from the polar fleece. The main cat patterns will be cut out from these pieces of material.

Helpful hints

If in doubt, always draw your pattern or guidelines onto fabric before cutting, and pin pieces together before stitching them. It is easier to avoid mistakes than to rectify them.

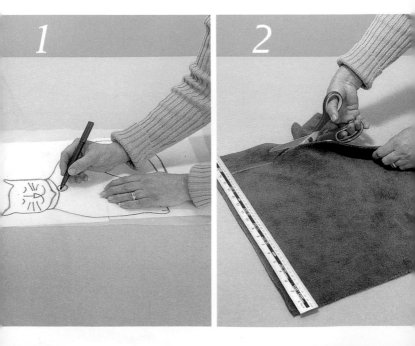

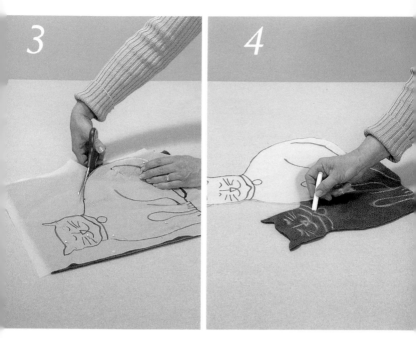

3 Place the tracing paper patterns over the rectangles of fleece fabric, smooth them both out, and then pin them carefully together, positioning the pins within the outline of the cat. Once you are satisfied that the pattern is smoothly and securely attached to the rectangle of fleece, use your scissors to cut carefully around the outline of the cat, through both the tracing paper and the fleece.

4 Chalk the cat's facial features, collar, legs, and tail carefully onto the fleece. Overlay the tracing paper pattern onto the fleece to check the accuracy of your drawing.

5 Sew the features onto the fleece fabric, by either sewing machine or hand, using a small piece of black cloth for the cat's nose. Set your sewing machine to a close zig-zag stitch for this part of the project. Alternatively, you can satin stitch the cat's features and whiskers.

6 Once you have attached the nose and sewn the other features, carefully trim away the excess black material from around the nose to leave a neat, triangular, feline-looking muzzle.

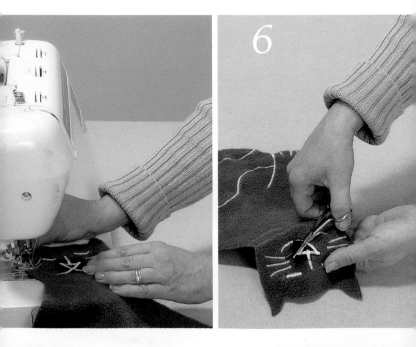

7 Cut out shapes for the cat's collar and tag from different colored scraps of fabric and satin stitch them carefully onto the main shape, following the chalked lines that you drew onto the fabric earlier. Before you begin sewing, double-check the dimensions of each little feature against your original tracing paper drawing if you are not satisfied with the size or shape of any item. Either satin stitch the eyes or use buttons if you prefer.

8 Iron the stiff backing onto the cat pattern. Iron around the outline first and then set the iron to "steam"/"hot" to bond the backing securely onto the cat. Once the backing is fully attached, pull off the backing paper.

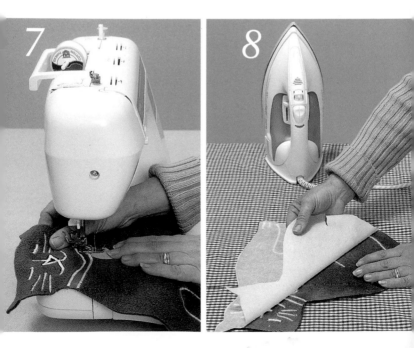

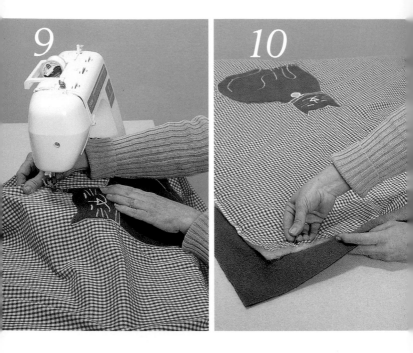

9   Place the cat in position on the bed cover and iron the whole design over thoroughly until it sticks to the material. Once the backing webbing has melted and the design is securely stuck to the bed cover, sew around the edges of the cat design to complete its attachment to the bed cover.

10   Pin together the bed cover gingham (with the cat pattern now attached), the wadding, and the fleece. Ensure that the fleece backing of the bed cover overlaps the edges of the gingham and wadding by a minimum of 2 in. all round.

11 Cut across the corners of the fleece backing at a 45-degree angle to miter them, and neatly fold down the edges.

12 Pin the fleece over onto the gingham all the way around, to form an edging to the bed cover. Then use red thread to sew around the folded back fleece and finish off the bed cover.

Helpful hints

This cat design can easily be modified to suit different tastes. Try alternative textures and colors to suit your child's preference—or go for a different animal altogether!

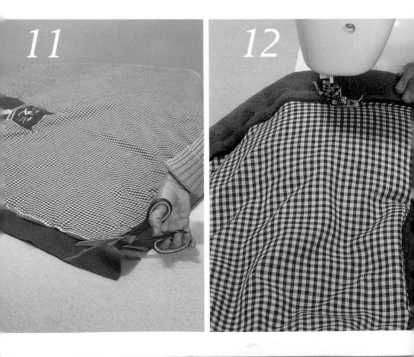

making a sheep- **shaped headboard**

Children adore themed furniture and playful everyday items in their rooms, and this charming, easy-to-make bed headboard in the shape of a sheep with a nuzzling lamb will delight the most style-conscious youngster. Licensed-character headboards can be expensive and garish, but this project offers an attractive alternative if you have a modicum of artistic ability and a little patience. However, be sure to check the adaptability of your child's bed-base before you embark on this project.

Materials

Bed headboard: 1 piece of MDF ¾ x 36 x 24 in.

Supports: 2 pieces of PAR 3 x 1 x 30 in.

White primer • Paint • Screws

Tools

Workbench • Paint brushes • Drill • Screws • Pencil • Metal straightedge • Combination square • Jigsaw • Abrasive paper

Skill level

Beginner

Time

4 hours

Easy home improvements

1. Photocopy the sheep template on page 109 of this book, enlarging it as much as possible on a sheet of foolscap paper. Place the sheet of MDF on a workbench. Draw out the grid pattern on the sheet of MDF and carefully copy the cutting pattern—that is, the outline of the entire sheep design—following the template square-by-square on the grid.

2. Once the design has been fully copied onto the sheet of MDF, use the jigsaw to cut out the outline of the sheep. Make smooth, sweeping cuts with the jigsaw, ensuring that you move the tool with your whole arm, right from the shoulder, and not just by moving your wrist. Move the sheet of MDF around on your workbench as necessary, to facilitate the cutting process and ensure smoother cut lines.

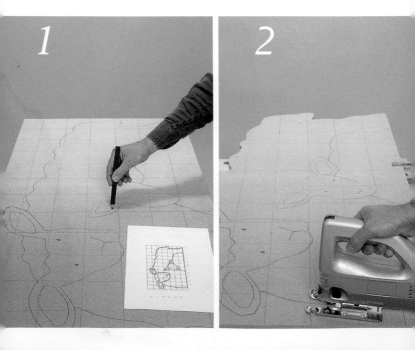

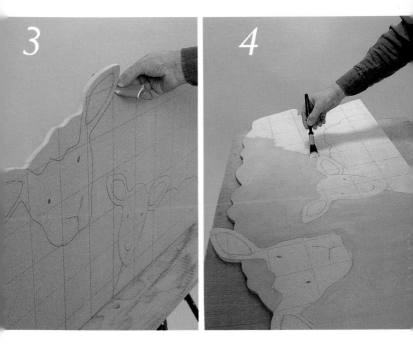

3 Use a sanding block and piece of abrasive paper to rub down the edges until they are smooth and make sure that any MDF splinters have been removed.

4 Take up your paper template and grid once more and carefully copy the painting pattern for the sheep and lamb to the MDF headboard. Follow the grid and mark clear outlines in pencil. Thoroughly dust off the headboard and then begin priming it with a proprietary undercoat and soft paint brush.

Helpful hints

When cutting and sanding MDF, always wear a face-mask that will cover the eyes, nose, and mouth. Thoroughly ventilate the room you are working in.

5 When the primer has dried thoroughly, begin painting in the sheep's face in brown and the lamb's body in cream. Follow the pencil outlines carefully and use the paint sparingly to avoid the likelihood of smudges and mistakes.

6 Next, take up a fresh brush and begin filling in the sheep's body, painting its wool in a swirling pattern to approximate the curls in a real sheep's fleece. Let some of the grey undercoat paint show through the white, swirling brush strokes that you make, as this will enhance the overall effect of "wool." Use more paint with some of the white strokes to vary the density of the curls and once more improve the overall look and texture.

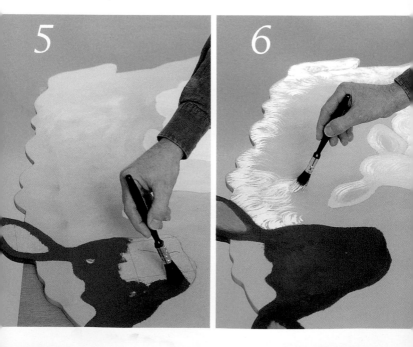

7 When you have completed the painting of the main sheep body, face, and lamb, allow the paint to dry thoroughly and then begin painting in the details of the design. Use a finer paint brush than before, and follow the original template and grid to ensure the correct placement of the sheep's and lamb's features.

8 Mark the positions of the two fixing battens on the reverse of the headboard. Drill and countersink two evenly spaced fixing holes in each batten. Attach the battens to the headboard using 1¼ in. (No. 6) screws. The position and length of the battens will be dictated by the reciprocal fixings on the bed-base to which you are attaching the bed headboard.

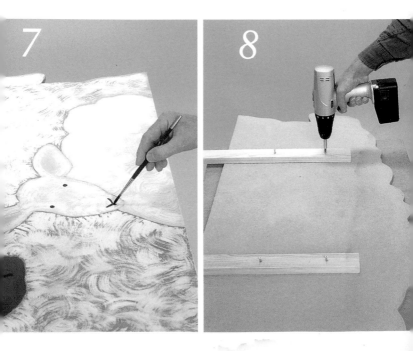

building a **doll's house**

The doll's house is one of the oldest and most traditional of all children's toys. If you choose one of quality, it is also one of the most expensive. How much more satisfying it would be to build your own . . . This project offers an attractive and viable alternative to seeking out the right domicile for your child's favorite toys, and does not demand too much difficult construction work.

Materials (all lumber is softwood unless otherwise stated)

Back: 1 piece of ply ¼ x 22 x 22 in.

Front: 2 pieces of ply ¼ x 7 x 15¾ in.

Floors: 2 pieces of ply ¼ x 9½ x 22 in.

Sides: 2 pieces of ply ¼ x 3 x 10 in.

Roof: (front) 1 piece of ply ¼ x 5 x 8 in.; (right side) 1 piece of ply ¼ x 5¾ x 10⅞ in.; (left side) 1 piece of ply ¼ x 5⅝ x 10⅞ in.

Frame: 16 ft. of 1 x 1 in. Ramin semi-hardwood

¾ in. veneer pins • No. 4 (¾ in.) brass screws and screw cups

Tools

Workbench • Miter saw • Power drill • Set-square • Coping saw • Hand saw • Hammer • Wood glue • Abrasive paper/sanding block

Skill level

Advanced

Time

8 hours

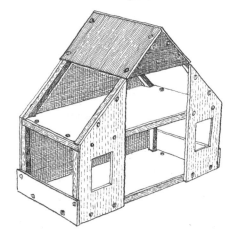

1 The doll's house will have a framed structure made up of Ramin joined battens. These will run along the edges of each wall of the house and across the front and back where the walls slope diagonally into the roof. To mark out the triangle of the roof frame, mark the height of the side walls in pencil on each side of the board (9 in.) and use an adjustable set-square to measure a 45-degree angle. Then, draw the two lines that make the triangle of the roof. Cut out the side, back, and front walls of the doll's house.

2 Draw the plan for the doll's house frame onto the back and front walls, using the width of wood strut that will be used, to make the plan precise. This will cover all the edges of the front and back walls and a strut across the center where the vertical wall slopes diagonally into the roof.

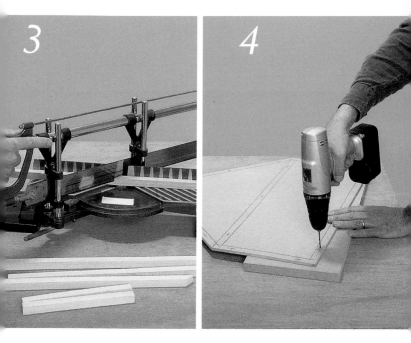

3 Mark and cut 45-degree miters on the ends of all the doll's house frame pieces, using a miter saw. Ensure that all the cuts are consistent with one another to guarantee tight, strong joints. Smooth off any splinters or rough edges with fine abrasive paper.

4 Once you have marked out the frame pattern, drill three evenly spaced pilot holes for each batten in the centers of the fixing guidelines on the back wall. These holes should be drilled to the width of the shank of a No. 4 (¾ in.) screw.

5 Screw the back wall of the doll's house to the Ramin wood frame using No. 4 (¾ in.) brass screws with screw cups to recess the heads of the screws. Ensure that everything lines up correctly and that the frame is square to the edge of the back wall.

6 Mark out the windows on both the sides of the doll's house facade. Drill out the corners of the marked-out window using a ¼ in. drill bit to make a hole big enough to take the blade of a coping saw. Drill accurately and be careful not to allow the drill-hole to break too far on either side of the pencil line marking out the window.

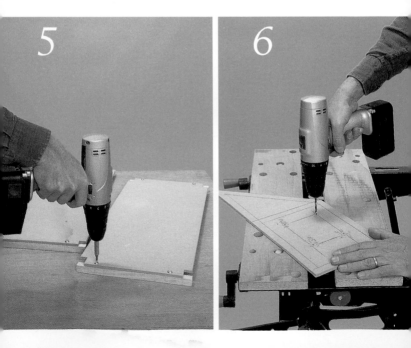

7   Unscrew the blade of a coping saw and insert it through one of the uppermost window corner holes you have just drilled. Saw downward, carefully following the pencil outline of the window, until you reach the corner hole beneath the one you have sawed down from. Hold the top of the doll's house side to steady it as you saw, if you prefer.

8   Assemble the front wall of the doll's house, using No. 4 (¾ in.) brass screws with screw cups, driven into the pilot holes that were drilled in the MDF wall in step 4 and into the Ramin wood frame. As you assemble the front wall, periodically place it over the back wall that has already been made, to ensure that the two walls line up perfectly with one another.

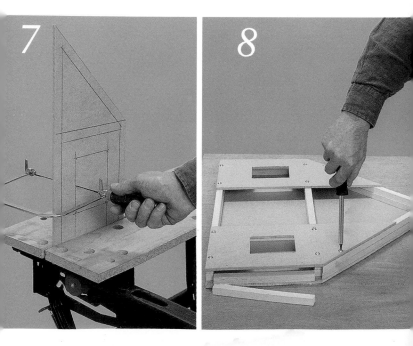

9   Take the two pieces that make up the floors of the doll's house and offer them up to the assembled back and front of the house. Mark rebates on the corners of both floors, carefully aligning them with the Ramin frame that they will fit into. The rebates will need to be cut out of the corners before the floors can be assembled to the rest of the house.

10   Prior to fitting the last bits of panelling to the house frame, sand off all edges to ensure that there are no splinters or rough areas that could damage a child's soft hands. Once all edges are properly smooth, dust off the floor panels before fixing them into the doll's house frame.

11 Fix the doll's house floors to the front, back, and sides, once more using No. 4 (¾ in.) brass screws with screw cups to recess the heads of the screws. Check the fixings carefully to ensure the correct alignment of all joints. Turn the doll's house over on the workbench to facilitate fixing all walls into the floors.

12 Finally, attach the MDF side walls and the doll's house roof, using the same brass screws and cups as for the rest of the structure. Check for all-around fit, sand as necessary, and then paint or varnish the doll's house according to your preference.

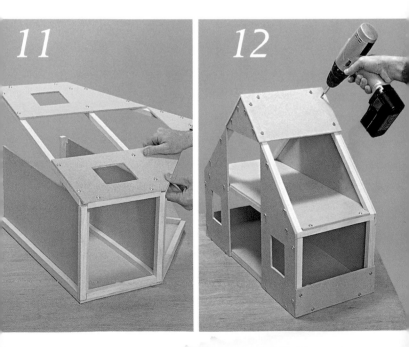

101

making a
fun mirror frame

Frames brighten up ordinary mirrors and walls, and this brightly colored, fun wooden frame in the shape of a television set would enliven any children's room wall. The project is relatively simple to make and does not require either special tools or skills. The most important thing is to ensure that you buy a good mirror to fit and that it is then safely secured within the television-screen frame. Then the next time your child asks to watch television, you can send them to their bedroom instead!

Materials

Sheet of ½ in. MDF • 2 x 1 in. construction lumber • 1 in. dowel • Mirror 14½ x 18½ in. • Chain • Mirror fixings • Selection of brightly-colored acrylic paints • 2 screw-in eyelets • Panel pins • Wood glue

Tools

G-clamp or workbench with integral clamp • Jigsaw • Hand saw • Hammer • Abrasive paper • Paint brushes

Skill level

Beginner

Time

4 hours

1 Cut a rectangle of 24 x 18 in. MDF. This will be the front board of the television mirror frame. Using a pencil, rule, and round cup or saucer for the corners, draw out a television "screen" on the MDF sheet, to dimensions of 18 x 14 in.

2 Complete your marking out by measuring everything once more and ensuring that the "screen" is properly centered on the front board overall. Make any corrections in pencil and satisfy yourself that the shape of the screen is even and centered before beginning to cut out of the MDF board.

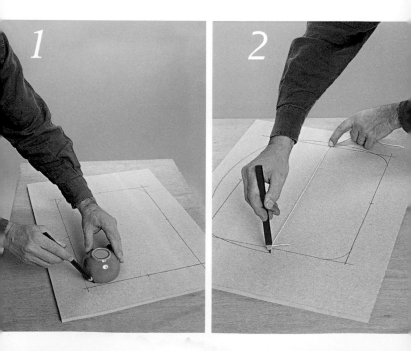

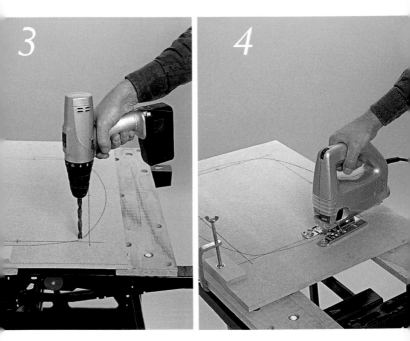

Clamp the board to a workbench and select a drill-bit large enough to make a hole that will take a jigsaw blade. A width of ½ in. should be sufficient. Drill a hole carefully into one rounded corner of the television "screen." Be careful not to let the drill-hole break beyond the outside of the pencil line marking the corner of the screen.

Insert the blade of your jigsaw into the hole and slowly begin to saw out the shape of the television "screen," following the pencil line around the MDF board. Keep the board clamped to a workbench for stability, but stop sawing periodically, and adjust the position of the board to facilitate your cutting. Be careful not to cut into your workbench.

5 Clamp a length of dowel into your workbench and saw off four 1-in. lengths for use as "television control knobs." Make sure the knobs are all cut evenly and sand off any rough edges or splinters.

6 Cut four pieces of 2 x 1 in. lumber to the following dimensions: two lengths of 24 in.; two lengths of 16 in. These four pieces of wood will make up the mirror frame.

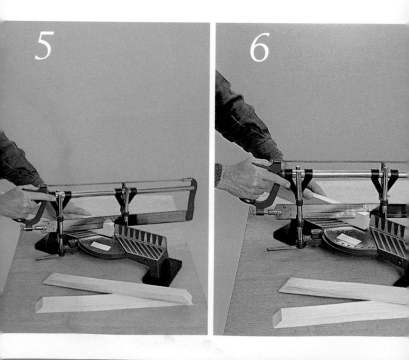

7 Mark, glue, and pin the pieces of 2 x 1 in. wood to the back of the MDF front board, fitting the two longer lengths along the sides and the shorter lengths at the ends. Be careful not to use too much glue, to avoid spillage down the sides of the mirror frame.

8 Sand the mirror frame as necessary and then paint the front and frame sides in a bright, primary color. Paint the control knobs in different colors for added fun. Glue the knobs to the front board. Fit the mirror into the back of the frame using fixings according to the manufacturer's instructions. Finally, use ½ in. screws to attach a chain to the top of the back frame from which to hang the mirror on the wall.

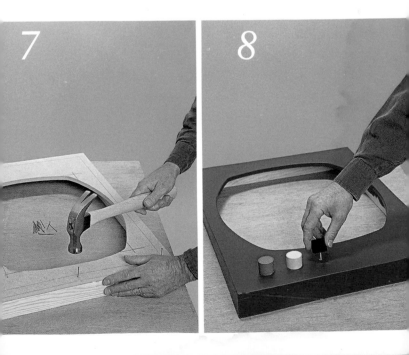

Daisy stencil template (pp 10–15)

Roller blind sun template (pp 32–39)

Roller blind moon template (pp 32–39)

Appliqué-cat bed cover template (pp 80–87)

1 2 3 4 5 6 7 8 9 10 11 12

eep-shaped
dboard template
88–93)

glossary

Batten—a narrow strip of wood, often used to describe such a strip used as a support for other pieces

Bevel—any angle other than a right angle at which two surfaces meet

Butt joint—a simple joint where two pieces of wood meet with no interlocking parts cut in them

Clearance hole—a hole drilled to the width of the screw shank, through which a screw passes before entering a pilot hole (*cf.*)

Countersink—to cut, usually drill, a hole that allows the head of a screw, nail, or pin to lie below the surface

Hardwood—wood cut from trees like oak, cherry, and elm, belonging to the botanical group *Angiospermae*

MDF—medium-density fiberboard; a prefabricated material that can be worked like wood

Miter—a joint made by cutting equal angles, usually

at 45 degrees to form a right angle in two pieces of wood; cutting such a joint

PAR—"planed all round"; timber that has been planed smooth on all sides

Pilot hole—a small-diameter hole drilled into wood to act as a guide for a screw thread

Rebate—a stepped, usually rectangular, recess, cut along the edge of a piece of wood as part of a joint

Ripping—sawing wood along the grain

Softwood—wood cut from trees like pine, maple, and cedar, belonging to the botanical group *Gymnospermae*

Stencil—a transferable ink or paint pattern

Template—a cut-out pattern on paper or cardboard, used to help shape wood or transfer a pattern (*cf.* stencil)

Upright—a vertical piece of wood, usually part of a frame

index

acknowledgments

All photographs taken by Alistair Hughes, except for:

8/9 Elizabeth Whiting Associates; 40/41 Houses and Interiors;
78/79 Camera Press Ltd.

Illustrations by Stewart Walton.